The
Greatest
Internet Networker
In The World

Stories On How People Used
The Online Marketing Strategies
To Become The Most Successful Upline
In The World

Terms and Conditions

Table Of Contents

Forward

Chapter 1:
The Beginning

Chapter 2:
About Being Real

Chapter 3:
A Secret And Treasure

Chapter 4:
The Bigger Picture

Chapter 5:
Teaching Others

Chapter 6:
The Right Questions

Chapter 7:
Life Lessons

Chapter 8:
Imaging And Teaching

Wrapping Up

Foreword

Here is the chronicle of a young man on the brink of resigning the business, who distinguishes that the secrets of MLM success lie inside him. It's a tale that's altered a lot of lives.

It starts at an opportunity meeting, where the storyteller meets amazing networkers.

Over the course of a week, the storyteller's life is metamorphosed as he soaks up lessons about leadership, beliefs, values and life purpose, hearing, championing other people, and more.

This is more than a feel-good story.

It's a first-hand, inside the Sojourner Truth about success in Network Marketing, this book has the might to really alter your life and raise your business to the greatest level.

And, beyond Networking, it's about fresh properties of productivity and fulfillment in each area of life... explaining how to undergo successful living along with successful network marketing.

Study it and truly understand what it feels like to be a Networker.

The Greatest Internet Networker In The World

Stories On How People Used The Online Marketing Strategies To Become The Most Successful Upline In The World.

Chapter 1:

The Beginning

Synopsis

I'll never forget this. The night I first met the leading networker.

The hotel room was jammed, as was common. When I walked in, I observed a particularly large swarm of individuals gathered around somebody in the front of the room. I took aside a distributor I'd met previously, pointed to the group and inquired, "Who's that over there?"

She said, "That's the Greatest Networker you'll ever meet ... Would you like to meet him?"

"Certainly," I said. She took me over.

The Lessons Begin

He was listening intently to what a woman standing directly in front of me was talking about, when his eye caught mine. He looked me directly in the face, extended his hand to me, and stated, with a warmth that really shocked me: "Hello. It's truly great to see you." He told me his name and asked me mine.

I stuttered – really, I bumbled. His grip became a little firmer and he asked, "How are you?" I said, "Fine, thanks". And he responded, "Truly?" Before I had time to stop myself, I found myself telling him how I was truly doing. He heard me in a way I've never experienced previously. I really felt him listening to me. I told him how my business and my life were going and that I wasn't cut out for network marketing. He smiled and squeezed my hand again and asked, "Would you have a little time after the meeting to spend with me?" Before I could get to my "No", I heard myself say, "That would be excellent".

Following the formal part of the meeting was over and the groups of fresh distributors and their sponsors were departing together, he addressed me. He smiled at me with that same noticeable warmth as previously. "Come on", he stated, taking me by the arm and moving off through the door. "Let's get some caffeine and something to eat. Have you had supper?" He stated with a warm laugh that he could use something delicious. I agreed – laughing right along with him. It felt great to be with him. He'd surely altered the way I was feeling in an unusually short time. "So, what do you like to eat a lot?" he inquired. And before I could answer – he said, "It's an earnest question. What would you most love to eat – right now?"

I took in a deep breath and stated, "Italian". "Excellent!" he said. "Me too." As we journeyed to the restaurant, we made small talk. Really, I made small talk. He simply kept asking me questions. He just seemed so curious, so intrigued in me – and so easy to speak to. I likely told him more about my life in those 10 short minutes than I'd ever told anybody before.

We entered the restaurant with the captain' and the greatest networker appearing to be the very best of acquaintances; and I noticed smiling exchanges passing constantly between my host and a variety of waiters and clients. As we took our seats, I noticed, "You certainly live in a different domain than I do." "How's that?" he inquired.

"Well, everyone is all grins and warmth and friendship . . . you appear to know everyone, and they all know you and like you. " Tell me", he inquired, "what's present for you when all of this 'grinning and friendshipping,' as you call it, is going on?" I inquired, "What do you mean?"

"What's here, like in the air around us – what do you notice is present for you?" I took in a deep breath and answered thoughtfully. "I feel jealous," I told him and curious, also. I wish to understand how I may have my life be like this." "Tell me," he inquired", what do you truly want your life to be like?" So began a 2-hour supper. All he did was ask me questions. And all I did was to tell him principles I hadn't ever shared with anybody!

"Look, where's all of this going?" I inquired. "You're asking me questions and talking about things that nobody's ever said before. He didn't say a word – simply leaned forward, and turned his head toward me, as though he wanted to make certain to catch every syllable I spoke. I felt feelings well up inside me. Huge feelings. Crucial ones. I felt suddenly really sad. "I simply want to be a success," I told him. "I'm so tired of not having the cash to do what I want . . . to provide for my family. " But . . .?" he asked.

"But, I don't know how", I replied. Network marketing doesn't work for me. I looked over at him and inquired, "What's wrong with me?" He let his head fall back and consulted at the ceiling. He took a big, long, deep breath and asked, "How would you like me to show you how?" "Yes!" I cried out. "Good," he said. "We'll begin tomorrow. Here's what I wish you to accomplish . . ."

He handed me a sheet of paper with his address and told me to come to his office the next afternoon after I got off work. He reached into his briefcase and drew out a package. "Here," he stated, "this is your homework. I need you to study this before we meet tomorrow – all right?"

He paid for supper and drove me back to the hotel where the meeting had been. I watched him go then I went home. I opened the book with enormous excitement. I stopped cold. There wasn't a word in it.

Each page in the book was completely blank!

Chapter 2:

About Being Real

Synopsis

Time literally crept by that following day. I had to go to the meeting...I couldn't stand it any more.

When I got there the main house, it was simply splendid! As a matter of fact, this was the sort of house I'd always dreamed of having. And horses grazing in the fields. As I arrived at the paddock fence, I called the nearest of the horses. Just then, I observed a horse and rider coming out of the woods, cantering toward me. It was him.

Truth Lesson

The mare I'd called to and the keenest marketer reached me at the same time. "Well, you surely got her attention. She doesn't come to simply anybody. "It's great to see you. You're 60 minutes early," he noted. "How are you?" He walked over and extended his hand.

"I'm great," I replied", . . . and a bit anxious." He laughed, another one of those thundering laughs of his, and stated, "You do learn fast. Thanks for being so truthful. What are you anxious about?" "Well," I stated as I pointed in a sweeping motion that took in his property, "this isn't where I generally find myself on a Friday afternoon. This is a pretty amazing place you've got."

"You know," I told him, "I've a dream of owning a place much like this". "Great," he stated, "would you like to purchase it?" "I doubt it's inside my budget at the minute," I stated, sarcastically. "I don't recall stating how much I'd sell it for – did I?" "No", you didn't." "So how do you know whether or not it's inside your budget?" he inquired. "All right", I sighed. "How much?" "2.6 million", he expressed flatly. "Do you wish to purchase it?"

"Stop it!" I took a firm stand. "This is absurd. You know I don't have that sort of cash!" "I don't know that," he stated. "And that's not what I inquired. I inquired if you wished to purchase it. Do you – yes or no?" "This is senseless," I snarled. He stuck up his hand – I quit talking. "Yes or no?" he asked once more. "Do you wish to purchase my house?" "No. Don't be idiotic," I stated. "I'm not being idiotic," he said. "But – you are! Among the most idiotic things an individual can do is to not tell the truth." "You're lying," he stated sternly. "Please," he said, "tell me if what I'm about to say is true or not: you'd love nothing more in this world than to purchase my house. I'm asking merely if you'd like to purchase my house – yes, or no?" "Well, if you put it that way – yes, I'd like to purchase your house."

He smiled. "I do put it that way," he said. "Tell me, do you frequently have trouble answering the questions individuals ask you?" "Well . . ." I began, but then shook my head and went silent. I looked up at him, attempting to read something from his face – desiring to find the correct answer there someplace. "There's no correct answer," he stated, as if reading my mind. "There's only your answer, today, to the question."

We stood in hush for some time. When I finally got up the courage to look at him, he stated, "Look, in our relationship together, I take a firm stand that you and I speak the facts. I believe that will be hard for you, as you don't listen, not yet. What you hear me stating is colored by what you say to yourself about what I'm saying. Is that true?"

"Yes," I told him. He nodded and carried on. "Did you study the book I gave you?" I didn't know what to say. How do you study a book without a word in it? "Yes or no?" he inquired, with patience.

"Sure," I said. "Well, what did you think?" "I'm not sure . . ." "Great!" he shouted. "Come up to the house and tell me all about it."
 I wasn't sure what to think. So, for the minute, I attempted to think nothing, and just watch where I was going.

Chapter 3:

A Secret And Treasure

Synopsis

The home and its surroundings were even more impressive from a closer look. Everything was simply magnificent. Individuals actually lived here – and as if to prove it, 3 bounding dogs merrily greeted me as I got out of my automobile.

"Oh, you've been properly greeted, I see", the he said, as he came through a door in a high stone wall. "Might I introduce you to Mr. and Mrs. Silver?" He patted the heads of a big, fine-looking pair of silver standard poodles. "And this is the Duchess", he stated, ruffling the fur of a Border Collie. He said, "Come to my office".

His office was comfy and lived in. "You've got quite a library", I noted. It was an understatement in the extreme. "Yes," he stated, surveying what must have numbered well over a 1000 books. "I like books. I love info of all kinds – do you?" +

"Info?" That was a curious way to put it. "Certainly," I stated. "So tell me", he inquired, "What did you think about the book I gave you to study?" "Of all the books I've ever read – that's the most crucial book of all."

Behind The Mystery

I searched his face to distinguish his expression. I questioned if he were kidding . . . if he may be playing with me. He was looking straight at me open, expressionless. "Well . . . I don't know," I stated. "Great," he responded. "Perfect." I didn't understand what to say.

"There's a tale I wish to tell you," he stated. "Would you care to hear it?" "Certainly." "In Japan, a lot of years ago, it was the tradition amid Buddhist monks to move from monastery to monastery, looking for the teaching of the masters. As was the custom, the master would serve up tea and they'd talk. "One young monk was an especially outstanding pupil. " One day, he went to a really famous monastery attached to one of the most hallowed temples in Japan. The young man solicited an audience with the master, in hopes of being accepted as his student.

"The young man was showed to the master's chambers at once." The master came in and they bowed to one another. "The young man told the master of his travels, of the teaching he had heard, of the monks he had 'bested' in his hunt for Truth. The master heeded intently and recognized the young monk for his wit and intelligence.

The master started pouring tea for them both. The young man turned to the Master: 'I wish to stay here and learn with you, for I sense that here, contrary to with the others, there's much you have to provide me . . .' suddenly, the young monk exclaimed out in pain , jumping up from the floor . The blistering hot tea had splattered all over his lap!

"The master sat sedately and continued streaming tea – which was overflowing the student's little cup and spilling over the table onto the floor where the young man had been seated. " What are you doing, I have been burned! Quit pouring! The cup is brimming over!'

"Depart from me, young man," the master stated. 'I've nothing to teach you. Your cup is overflowing with all that you know and all that you believe you don't know. Return to me when your cup is void and you're ready to experience what I have to give."

We sat in hush for a while.

Finally, he spoke up. "You want a great deal to be a success in Network Marketing, don't you?" "Yes," I replied. "You understand some things about how to do this business – right?" "Yes." "And you understand, too, that there are a lot of things that you don't know about – right?"

"Yes," I responded. "There's nothing which you now understand, and nothing about what you believe you don't understand, that will help you produce the success you want." "The key to your success dwells in what you don't understand that you don't understand. Do you understand?"

No," I told him honestly. "I've no clue what you're saying. How may I understand what I don't even understand that I don't understand?" "You can't," he stated. "That's the mystery."

When I viewed my watch, it was a little past 1:00 a.m. We'd been talking for nearly 6 hours. The whole conversation had been about me – my past, present and future. I was left with a feel of enormous peace – and freedom. I felt someway more hopeful and really alive.

Throughout our talk, he would ask me if such and such were among my values- those crucial qualities that were most significant to me. "Values come in pairs, one providing for the manifestation of the other, he stated. Just one by itself is incomplete . . ."

"Hold off!" I interrupted. "You mean, always? How come in pairs?" He appeared to like the interruption. "Excellent question!" he beamed. "Tell me: do you understand why you've two eyes?" "Bifocal vision . . . depth perception," I said.

"Correct! Very good. It doesn't appear like we'd truly need 2, does it? Either eye works fine on its own. However working together as a pair, they add to 'vision' the depth perception. "And one eye 'anchors' the vision of the other". "It's the same with your values. One affirms the other. Together, they let your vision operate in depth."

"Look at what you were just telling me. Do you see how 'success' and 'freedom' are related for you?" I answered that I did. I remember telling him how much of my life, I'd felt ensnared . . . how without success, I felt like a captive.

"So you may say," he continued "that 'success,' for you, supplies for the expression of 'freedom.' That the one really gives the other a reference point, a context for its existence."

"Right, I see – they work together . . ."

As we carried on talking, I discovered additional sets of values I had: gratitude and recognition . . . adventure and play . . . communication and power . . . Assistance and contribution . . . partnership and leadership .There were others. These seemed the most crucial.

Then he inquired, "What is your life purpose?" That was the greatest question anybody had ever asked me.

I started envisioning a number of scenes: some funny ones, a few pitiful ones (from while I was growing up) – and a whole bunch of things I'd never accomplished before. It was awesome how many different and fantastic things were there!

"How did it all end?" he asked. "It was funny," I said. "It ended right here, right in this room. But rather than you sitting where you are now, I was sitting there. And there was a young woman sitting here where I am now, and I was inquiring about her life's purpose."

He shut his eyes and we sat in silence for some time. "So, what's your life purpose?" he inquired again.

"Teaching," I said. "I'm a teacher . . . and an author – and what I teach individuals is how to be successful and free. I show them how to accomplish their life's purpose. And", I added, "I make a profound difference in 1000s, even 1000000s of individual's lives."

I can't tell you what an extraordinary sensation I felt as I said those words.

Chapter 4:

The Bigger Picture

Synopsis

I spent that night in a guest room. It was rather late when we'd finished talking, and since he'd asked me to go to a training he was giving early the following morning, he asked me to stay the night.

As I was about to get ready for bed, I recognized that I hadn't phoned my wife! I found a telephone and called to let her know I wouldn't be home till the following day. She was really curious to understand what had occurred thus far – We hadn't talked like this in years.

Intriguing . . . I thought, as I hung up the telephone. I woke feeling more alive and happy than I'd been in years.

Secrets

I showered fast and went down the stairs. There was a fire in the hearth! On the couch was a bundle of clothes tied with a brilliant red yarn with a note on top. It stated: morning. Here are some clothes and sneakers for you. Hope they fit. Sneakers? For a training meeting?

I looked at the clothes, which turned out to be a bright colored jogging suit with a white polo shirt and gray rag-wool socks. This was going to be an unequaled meeting, I believed.

At 7 sharp, he walked through the door bearing a large tray. "Good day . . . good day. How are you?" "Brilliant", I responded. "How are you?" "Marvelous", he stated. "Have you seen the Peafowl?" "The peacocks?" I queried – and then replied, "Yes". "I've never been that close to one before. ' Amazing' isn't grand enough to describe them."

"Yes," he stated. "They're brilliant creatures. Walking flower gardens. Simply being around them is an unceasing reminder for me of the amazing possibility of beauty in our lives.

"Well," I asked, "tell me about this training session." He walked to his office, returned swiftly with a little paperback, and flung it to me. I caught it, turned it over and read the title aloud: Coaching Kids To Play Baseball and Softball. "There are many fine books on how to do Network Marketing and training," he said. "This is among the best." "Coaching Kids . . . ?" I inquired. "Yes", he answered. "Coaching Kids . . . "When I was first beginning," he said, "there weren't all the books and tapes we have now explaining how to do marketing successfully. The only thing I recognized was where not to look." "What do you mean?" I inquired. "Marketing is a whole different paradigm." "Pair o' dimes . . . Twenty cents. You know how we state, 'Here's my two cents,' when we're giving somebody our opinion or viewpoint? A paradigm is simply that – a viewpoint, a way we view things.

"The paradigm of marketing," he carried on, "is so basically different and distinguishable from all other paradigms of business, that it calls for a pretty complete shifting from the way we commonly view business to appreciate and comprehend it.

"For instance, in our industry, each company, regardless how different its products and services are, competes directly with every other marketing company in attracting individuals to their business opportunity. That sort of rivalry from every angle doesn't exist anyplace else – in any other industry.

"Now, given that unparalleled competitive environment, there's the tendency for individual distributors to say their opportunity is the best. " Woefully, most of them simply think to accomplish producing the perception of 'best' based on their old paradigm values – becoming the best by putting down the rivalry. However when net marketing distributors put down other companies, they're likewise putting down the industry at large.

"What occurs then – and remember, we're the 'word-of-mouth' business – is that there's this developing communication out there in the world about how foul this company is, and that company is, and this other company is." "Do you see where I'm going with all of this?" he inquired. In fact, I was now starting to feel a good-sized chunk of sorrow for all that negative talk I'd put out into the world.

He said, "We all – every single Networking distributor – have the responsibility to 'sell' our industry itself, as well as our private products and opportunity. That's what the word 'sponsor' means – being responsible for the individuals you bring into the business. "When you're responsible for an organization of 1000s of individuals, you bring in a lot of cash. Which is excellent. That's as it should be. "Right now, you're concerned with your endurance in this business, with your responsibility for producing your own success – right?" "Yes," I stated.

"All right. Now, what would be different if you were worried about the success of the whole industry? If that were your duty?" "Oh, wow . . ." I stated. "What would you spend your time centered on?" he inquired. "Making a point individuals knew the great news about Internet Marketing and thought really well of us.

Helping individuals understand how excellent this is. Abolishing abuses in the industry. Things like that," I stated. "Would you be at all worried about whether someone said 'Yes' or 'No' to trying out your products or joining your opportunity?" "No. I would not."

"And would that let you approach building your business differently than the way you've been executing it." "I got it!" I shouted. "By taking my focus and attention off myself, and placing it on something bigger, the issues I now think are huge get littler – immediately. They seem so easy now. I don't care about them any longer."

"Bingo!" he stated. "Have a goal bigger than you are. The greater the better. That way, you don't have time to sweat the little stuff.

Chapter 5:

Teaching Others

Synopsis

As we went out to the place where the training session was to happen, I asked him what it was like when he started. "The 1st couple of years I was in this business," he said", I got only a little success – at best.

"I began like gangbusters. I assembled a 'names list' of 250 individuals. "209 of them said 'Yes' and ordered the product – and I signed on fifty of them as distributors. Not bad, huh?" he stated. "Trouble was," he carried on", after 4 or 5 months, not one of them was doing the business!"

"What I was doing was working beautifully. For me. And not for them."

Instructing Others

"The one matter that was missing," he stated, "Was doing the business in a way that other people could easily do, too." "So, what did you do?" I inquired. "So, what did I do?" he spoofed. "So, I failed!" "That was my 1st huge lesson. Once I recognized what was missing, I set out to discover a way to do this business that anybody – of regardless what age, experience, background, gifts or whatever – could accomplish. And more significantly, what anybody could teach other individuals to do easily and effortlessly.

"And for that, I discovered that the kids were some of my best mentors." Ah, so that's where the kids come in, I contemplated.

Just then, we pulled into a parking lot behind a Little League baseball field. "Come on", he stated. "Your trainers are waiting." I spent the following hour watching and playing tee-ball. The children had an excellent time. So did I. And the very first thing they executed in their practice blew me away. All the children sat around on the bottom rail of the backstop, behind home plate. The keenest networker enthusiastically called out each one by name. They started their practice cheering for one another. That was it.

All the praise during the game was centered on how much they were improving over the week before. If they messed up, he'd stop what was happening and ask them, "What happened?" He'd ask, "What could you do differently next time?" Occasionally the kids didn't know what they'd done; then he'd ask, did anybody else recognize what happened? When he got an answer to that, he'd ask the kid if that were true – and what was a different way they may do it next time?

Initially this whole process appeared a bit strange to me. Why not just tell them? So, I pulled him away, and asked him about that. "What do you learn when you ask me a question and I provide the answer?" he asked me. I considered that, and then responded, "I learn the answer."

"Precisely," he said. "And of what use is that?" "Well, then I understand what to do," I stated. "And of what use is that?" he inquired. "Once I know what to do, I may do it", I answered.

"2 things are crucial here," he said. "First, when you attain the answer yourself, it's really different than when somebody else tells it to you. Its meaning's richer, and there isn't any doubt about whether or not the other individual is right. It's your answer. You own it. And you're much more likely to recall it when you discover yourself in a like situation again. "What's more", he carried on, "when you find the answer for yourself, you not only get the answer you were looking for, but you get trained in discovering answers. So, there's twice the advantage. "Recognizing the answer, having the answer, is a far cry from doing the answer – would you agree?"

He interrupted my thoughts to explain. "Have you ever heard anybody discuss goal-setting with the terms, 'Have . . . Do . . . Be . . . ?' Have the things you wish to have . . . Do the things you wish to do . . . Be the sort of individual you wish to be . . . ?" I nodded that I had.

"The way I've discovered that works best is to center on being first. Once you accomplish that, doing and having come naturally. If you approach it the other way around, you may spend a lifetime not achieving your goals. Being first is actually simpler, as being begins in your mind. Anybody may be anything, anytime he or she wishes."

Chapter 6:

The Right Questions

Synopsis

After we'd said bye to the children I inquired uneasily about being and achieving. He stuck up his hand and interrupted me, "Not so quick. We'll do that. But firstly, tell me – did you have fun?" "I certainly did," I cried. "That's excellent," he said. "Did you learn anything new?" "Yes," I stated. "What?" he inquired. "A bunch," I stated. "Asking the children what they did, instead of telling them – I drew a lot from that. I recall my favorite instructors in school: they were the ones who let me find things on my own."

"The teachers who told me 'do this' or 'do that,' or simply had us repeat and remember bored me to death." "The way had the kids acknowledge themselves first gives the children responsibility for themselves, for trusting in their own thoughts first. That was simply excellent."

He simply viewed the road and said, "Great!" Then he inquired, "And what results did you acquire?" "Results?" "Results," he echoed. "What results did you accomplish today?" "I showed a kid how to catch the ball." "That's excellent", he laughed. "So, you had fun . . . you learned something new . . . and you acquired results, too – correct?" "Yes," I said. "Kudos – you win!" Win at what? I questioned – and then I recalled the points from the Coaching Kids . . . paperback: fun, learning, development and growth – and winning, when conceivable. Snap.

Inquire

"Those are the 3 elements in achievement," he said. "You acquire results. You learn, grow and develop. And, you have fun. All 3 are needed. If any one is lacking, you don't have true achievement."

"And", he carried on, "that's why you don't need to center on scarcely results – with yourself or with your folks . . ." Aha! I thought – so this truly is Network Marketing. This is critical in building a Network Marketing business: No results – no money. No learning – you get lost. No fun – you resign, or burn out, or burn out and resign." "I see that," I stated. "That's because it's simply info," he confided. "Once you begin being that way . . . once you start to be achieving, then you'll do those matters achieving individuals do, and you'll have those things achieving individuals have."

"So, how do I achieve that?" I inquired.

Being, that's what we were going to discuss next. As we returned to his house, he turned to me and inquired, "Wish to freshen up?" I said, "Certainly". And he asked, "Have you ever got a Japanese bath?" "No," I told him honestly. "At least I don't believe I have." "It's my belief," he stated as we walked into the main house", that the Japanese are killing us in business, merely because they know about baths and we don't. I'm on a one-person campaign to establish the bath in America, so the U.S. May recover our position as the world leader." He turned and said, "I'm not kidding!"

And then he said, like Teddy Roosevelt charging San Juan Hill – "To the bath!" The bath was remarkable, as I anticipated.

The entrance to the room was a little foyer with benches and hooks for hanging up our apparel. He motioned me to sit on one of the little stools that was facing the wall. On the wall were 2 bands of hot and cold water taps. Beside the stools were wooden pails that held water. Each had a sort of primitive, hand-crafted ladle inside. He filled up his bucket up with warm water, dumped it over his head, and told me to do the same.

Then he got one of those natural sponges, squeezed some liquid soap and tossed the bottle over to me. He started to soap himself everywhere with the sponge. "It's intriguing that we Westerners go into the tub first," he stated", then we lather ourselves. The Japanese taught me to do it this way. It saves water. And knowing the Japanese, I'm certain it likewise has to do with being respectful of others, and of the water too. After all, only a Gaijin, unmindful and disrespectful to the water kami, would go in a tub all dirty." "Kami . . . Gaijin . . . ?" I questioned out loud.

"Kami are spirits in the Shinto religion. Virtually everything on earth – in Japan – has a spirit. And Gaijin stands for 'foreigner' in Japanese", he told me. Once he had finished lathering from head to toe, he filled his bucket once more and rinsed himself off 12 times. I followed. We went over and sat slowly down in the tub. I looked around. The whole room was filled up with a light. I imagined he likely didn't wish to talk at that minute but I mustered the courage to ask softly if he was willing to tell me about being.

"Sure", he stated, and began with a question. "Who are you?" After a minor eternity, I stated, "I'm the sum of all the experiences I've ever experienced . . . all I've considered in those experiences . . . and all anybody's ever told me about me and them." he said . . .

"Astonishing". "And do you understand what all of that – your thoughts and the thoughts of other people about you – tallies up to?" "My being?" I inquired and answered at the same time.

"Close," he stated. "It's what your sense of your being comes from . . . what produces how you be in any situation. It tallies up to your habits of belief. What a few individuals call your belief systems.
"Habits," he carried on", are things we believe or do without conscious tending . . . without being cognizant of them. The moment we're cognizant of what we're believing or doing, it's no more a habit. It's a selection. "So, may you see, we may alter our habits by arriving at witting choices?" he inquired. "Yes," I stated.

"So", he carried on, "we bear these habits of belief about ourselves, and the reason they're so crucial is that they control what we have, do and be in our lives".

He was still for some time. "The Buddhists instruct that life is suffering" and his voiced was filled up with a mighty emotion. "And I concur – to a point. What they don't instruct, is how unneeded it is. Being suffering, being anything, may be altered, if we literally put our minds to it. We simply need to alter our minds. And we do that day in and day out. We simply have to learn how to accomplish it by choice."

"Habits of belief are produced the same way as any other habits – merely by doing the same thing again and again till you don't consider it any longer. That implies, you may produce a fresh habit the very same way."

"All right," he stated. "So, if you accept what I've said so far as true, what's the beginning question you've got?" "How do you alter the habit?"

"Substitute it with a fresh one." "How?" "How'd you acquire the original?" he inquired, then answered the question himself. "You got it by bearing a thought about what you believed. Then another and another. Pretty soon, you didn't have to impart any more thoughts – your habit of belief was in place. You simply held it there, affirmed it, reinforced it, each time you added a little fresh input – a little experience, something you stated about that, something somebody else stated to you about it – that agreed with or could be added to that subsisting habit of belief."

"So," I stated, "you start replacing your existing habit of belief?"
"Correct. So you start replacing your prevailing habit of belief by bestowing fresh thoughts. Right?" "Right", he concurred. "What sort of thoughts?" Thoughts which are about the fresh belief you wish to have."
"YES!" he exclaimed. "How do you feel?" he inquired.

"Great!" I stated.

"Hey," he stated, "would you like to meet my loved ones?"

"Sure!" I stated enthusiastically.

Chapter 7:

Life Lessons

Synopsis

As we left the bath and entered the small dressing foyer, I observed that the clothes we'd worn were gone. In their place were 2 neatly folded piles of clothing. "What's that?" I inquired, pointing to the big piece of bright fabric he was holding. "It's a sarong," he stated. "Wish to try one?" "Sure", I said, a little hesitantly. He demonstrated 2 different ways of tying the sarong. I selected the one I liked best. Following his measured directions, I wrapped it around me.

As we were walking back through the home, I inquired, "How did our clothes get there? I didn't hear anyone come in." "Likely, Rachel – that's my wife. But it could have been my daughter. Or Kazuko. She's the woman who attends to us."

I turned to see a little Japanese woman, bowing to me, her hands on her thighs. She leaned forward and smiled. She danced down the steps and marched over to me in long strides, nearly bounds. Stuck out her hand and said, "Hi. I'm Kazuko. It's a pleasure to meet you." I said hello, and added that it was a pleasure to meet her, too.

We talked a bit, the 3 of us. I turned and asked Kazuko how she had come to meet this great marketer and to live here with the family. "I met him in Japan. He was starting Network Marketing efforts in Japan and I met him at his very beginning meeting there.

Caring

"I was working as a housekeeper in the home of a rich businessman and his family. Both the mother and father had been educated in the U.S. In fact, that's where they met – and where I met them both." "Were you all at the same school here?" I inquired. "Yes," she stated." What college?" I inquired. "Yale," she stated. "What were you learning?" "I was on a cultural exchange program where drama majors were sent back and forth from Yale to Tokyo University," she replied. "That feels odd to me," I said. "You went to Yale, then returned to Japan and became a housekeeper?"

Kazuko laughed. "Yes, I'm certain it does. But truly, I'm really happy keeping a house and being part of a family. My kids are grown, with kids of their own now and I'm really devoted to this family. I've adopted them."

We carried on – I have no idea for how long. She was among the easiest individuals I had ever talked with. She told me about when the keenest networker first came to Japan, about that beginning opportunity meeting, and how really excited she had been at the idea of working with him.

Kazuko explained that the meeting had turned into a seminar on net marketing, that my new acquaintance had merely answered each question they asked, and that he had showed and told them all of his thoughts about how the business worked better. "Individuals were blown away," she stated. "They had never met somebody who was so enlightened and so willing to share his mysteries. Some individuals with other companies asked if they could sign up with him, but he really discouraged them! He told them to remain with what they were doing, and proposed to help them whenever and however he may.

"It was a noteworthy evening," she said. And then she added, "It surely altered my life." "How so?" I inquired. "There were a number of high-powered businessmen there", she answered. "Each one wished to be 'in charge' of Japan for him. He was really courteous to all of them, but he asked them, please, to wait. He explained that his company's chairperson would arrive the next week, and that he'd be the one to decide precisely what structure they'd utilize and who'd direct what efforts.

"Nearly everybody made an appointment to meet with him. I remained till the very end of the meeting and waited till there was no one else left. I went up to him and stated, 'Have you scheduled any time to see Japan?' He told me that he had reserved the following 3 days for that very use. I inquired if he would permit me to be his guide, and he stated he'd like that.

"So, the following morning, bright and early, we met at his hotel for breakfast. It was a whirlwind tour." She told me about all the places they traveled to. Kazuko told me that she'd never been to so many places in her own country in such a short time period in her life.

As they walked around, they had come across this one glorious home she had ever seen. Kazuko had told him then that this was just the sort of home she'd always dreamed of living in. She remembered how he had asked if she'd like to purchase the home, and how she'd jeered at his question, stating she could never afford such an amazing place! "I've had the same discussion with him about this place," I told her.

"Ah, so?" she inquired. "Well, take great care with what you dream, my friend. I've lived in that house in Nara for 6 years now." I sat agaze at her for a while. At last, she broke the silence, stating, "Close your mouth now. Flies will get in."

When they finally returned to Tokyo, she carried on, as they were sitting in his suite at the Imperial Hotel, he'd inquired what would she do to found a Network Marketing business in Japan. Whom would she pick to direct the work – with whom did she believe and feel would she wish to work? – By whom would she wish to be sponsored? "It was so much more of a question than I could answer, then" she said. "I recognized that it was awfully important to him, but I truthfully felt that any one of the businessmen at the meeting may be a fine choice, and I told him so.

"We talked for hours," she said", in fact, well into the following morning. We discussed what I thought would work best in Japan, about how Japanese individuals worked and lived, and what I thought they treasured most and wanted in their lives. I kept attempting to get him to tell me what he thought, but he simply wished to know my answers." We laughed, and as we did, he returned to the room and sat in a chair facing Kazuko and me. "So", he inquired, "did Kazuko illuminate you?"

"She was telling me how you met. How you started your Networking business in Japan. And how you never let her ask you any questions – which sounded pretty familiar to me", I said. He laughed and asked, "Did she tell you she was in charge of our Network in Japan?" "No," I stated with surprise. "She didn't!" "Kazuko-san", he scolded. "Tell him the truth." "He selected me to be in charge of our Japanese operations," she stated directly. "He caught a lot of flak for that –

initially. Anyhow, he told them I was the best individual. I understand they argued a lot about it . . ." "No, we didn't", he interrupted. "I merely made them a deal that was in their best interests."

"Oh, yes – you surely did that." She laughed, addressed me and stated, "He told them to afford me the position for one year, and that if I didn't exceed their sales and distributor goals – by a hundred percent! – he would sign over his commission back to the company for the next 12 months!"

"Tell the man what the sales goal was, Kazuko." "To reach $500,000 a month in Japan by the end of the first year," she stated. "And tell what you really achieved", he nudged. "No, you tell him, Gaijin-san." "Our little housekeeper here", he informed me", was the most successful distributor in the history of the company – worldwide. Her group did just under $11 million in total sales their 1st year. Kazuko became a millionaire before the end of her 2nd year in the business."

"Incredible!" I puffed, and they both laughed. "My friend", he said, "In this business, you'll only accomplish what your habits of belief allow. I chose Kazuko as I saw that she trusted anything was possible. She had no limitations in her paradigm for net marketing in Japan. She had none for herself, either. She didn't believe that it couldn't be done – and she declined to hear to anybody who told her differently."

She stated, "My dear friend here spent virtually every waking hour of each day with me for almost 6 months to get our business going. All I did was follow him around, translate and accomplish what he taught me. "That in itself was among the heftiest lessons I learned. And I've now done that with all my key individuals", she imparted.

"He told me that every highly successful net marketer he had ever met had brought in the bulk of his or her income from the sales yielded by 2 to 5 individual distributor groups built by leadership distributors. He said to seek those 4 or 5 individuals – to ask all my new individuals right up front if they were dedicated to accomplishing that level of leadership and success, and he told me to center my efforts on developing those people who had made that dedication. So I did."

"What about individuals who didn't wish to make that sort of commitment?" "I gave individuals what they wished," she stated. "Remember, I'm a housekeeper. I attend to people. So, I merely provided individuals the level of support and gave them the time and tending that was suitable for where they were and what they wished to achieve. But I was really clear about what I wished. I wished leaders who'd duplicate themselves. A number of my leaders now were individuals who had no clue they were capable of such things when they started."

Well, I sat back into the sofa. I'd heard all of this previously. Read it in books and interviews in networking publications. But I'd never sat opposite somebody who'd really accomplished it. My habits of belief were getting a true unfolding lesson here.

"Network marketing is all about taking care of individuals, and I like attending to individuals. You haven't met Rachel, yet. You will – he will, yes?" she inquired him. "I trust so," he replied, "though I'm not certain where she is. Have you seen her today, Kaz?"

"May we finish our talk about habits?" I inquired. "Let's!" he stated. "But first – know that previously there were 2 things I found which were missing in my being able to spend time in my life where I truly wanted."

"As soon as I started to observe my commitments, what turned up directly was how little freedom I had with my job to make fresh ones." "I believed I was a big deal. You know, 6-figure salary, all the advantages, called the shots. After all, I had my own business and I was the boss. Incorrect! "In reality, I was aghast when I saw how little freedom I really had." "And that's where Network Marketing entered the picture. I chose a company with a brilliant reputation – one which had been around long enough for the unparalleled ups and downs of this business to make them strong, which had strong management with field experience, an great product line consumers enjoyed once they tried and would continue to utilize forever, so there was residual income involved – and, the very best sponsor.

"In fact, the sponsor I desired," he carried on dramatically", was the dandiest networker in the world." "Stop!" I cried. "Hold off just a minute. I thought you were the greatest networker ever!" "Yeah, some individuals say that", he admitted. "But if that's true, what does that make the individual who taught me everything I know about this business?" There's an even better Networker than he is? I looked over at him, and then at Kazuko, and they simply sat there grinning, like 2 kids just barely keeping a secret. No answers there.

"All right . . ." I stated, expecting to say more, but nothing sprang to mind or mouth.

"Come on", he stated. "Let's go find my sponsor." It's her! I thought. It's has to be his wife, Rachel. "This is astonishing!"

Chapter 8:

Imaging And Teaching

Synopsis

We walked across the flagstone parking area in front of the home, and on down to the horse barn. Standing in front – clad in the boots, riding britches, blazer and white blouse of an equestrian – was Rachel. She looked and walked over to me. Stuck out her hand, and said, "I'm Rachel.

We'd gone back to the living room and Rachel came in. Rachel sat down next to me on the couch. "I like him", she informed her husband, and she smiled over at me. "Where'd he come from?" she asked no one particularly.

"We met Thursday evening at the meeting in town," stated my host. "I asked him to come to visit Friday, and we've been together since." "So", Rachel turned to me, "what have you been doing?"

"I truly don't know where to start. I tried my best to report on all the things we'd said and done. As I did, I realized what a massive amount of info, thought, fresh ideas and experiences I been open to – all in less than twenty-four hours.

Trusting And Teaching

Tell me", she inquired, "What's next for you?" "The place to begin," I started", is to build habits of belief which support my goals." "Smart boy – captivating boy", she stated to her husband.

"So, where will you start?" "Ah", I contemplated aloud, "with my goals – and a few general habits of belief I already recognize will support whatever I decide to accomplish". "Want a suggestion?" she inquired. "Certainly", I sounded out. "Play with your belief habits firstly."

"All right," I stated, slowly. "I think that my habits of dis-belief affect my power to produce my goals realistically – and by that I mean without the limits of what I've thought was conceivable. The kinds of habits I have today – or at least, have had, till today – have gotten me to where I am today. So, they obviously require a little work, as I'm not where I wish to be. "So," I continued", first step – balance, or begin to balance my life.

"All right," said the 2nd keenest networker, leaning forward from his seat", and how is that accomplished?" "That's my query for you – both," I stated, and I sat back, waiting to see what arrived next.

Rachel inquired, "So, we were discussing your habits of belief . . . Having to balance the scales with fresh habits . . . and you were about to ask us how that was done – correct?" "Yes," I stated. "Well", Rachel answered, "I'd like to hear what you'd do, first". "All right", I stated, by now not at all surprised that the issue had been quickly dropped back in my lap. "I'd have a look at my life. I'd take some from that and build beliefs, fresh, favorable habits of belief around that."

Simply know that because of all the old habits you've formed over the years, these fresh ideas and images might seem silly to you now, she said. "Well," I stated, closing my eyes to bring to mind an image of me standing on the stage in front of that applauding crowd.

"What were you doing just now?" "Well," I told her, "I was conjuring up the picture and looking at it". "Fantastic!" she proclaimed. "Why so fantastic?" I asked. "Because getting that picture in your mind, is precisely the process you utilize to alter any habit of belief you have on any matter, anyplace, anytime." "Even though these images are imagined, your brain accepts them as though they were real, as though they were actual experiences you've had and were merely recalling." "See what I'm saying . . . ?" Odd, I really did see what Rachel was saying.

At last I stated, "This is it – isn't it? This is how you form different habits – mental habits of belief that support you in producing what you wish in your life. Astonishing." "Yes, it is," Rachel stated.

As we were leaving the kitchen, the keenest networker turned to me and inquired, did I play billiards?" Pool?" I inquired in return. "No, billiards", he answered. "No pockets. Three balls. Two white – one red." I stated I'd never played, though I'd seen tables like that before and had wondered about the game. He took me through another part of the house to a fantastic room. The table itself was an antique. He concisely explained the object of the game to me. As we took our shots, we spoke about all sorts of things. I inquired if he and Rachel shot together and he said they had. I asked who was the better shot and he said he was. I asked if he meant to teach Rachel to be better than he was – and he said, "Nope". We played and talked for another hour or so." Billiards is really a lot like Network

Marketing," he said "In many ways." "It's a game of placement. Of course the shot right in front of you is crucial, but you have to likewise think ahead two, three shots or more. You need to make the first one successfully, but you're forever planning for the next one." That likewise builds momentum. And when you approach your business-building from that bigger perspective, your priorities switch and you start to center on longer-term concerns." "Like?" I asked him. "Teaching teachers is a great illustration," he told me.

"Commonly, when you're centering on teaching individuals to teach individuals, your results are slower in coming than if you centered on merely teaching individuals how to sell products and sponsor people. That's a simpler job, and it yields bigger results faster in terms of yielding sales income – at least at first. "But when you teach individuals to teach people, you move from producing results to empowering other people.

"Once I came to comprehend how the business works, that it depends upon our ability to effectively sponsor individuals who know how to teach people how to teach others, my business started to grow for real." "For the most part, you'll be working with beginners, turning them into pros. And, 'pro whats?' is a good question. Pro teachers."

"Naturally, you have to teach individuals to use the products and recommend them passionately to other people, and they have to know the high points of the compensation plan, and most especially, to have a deep, abiding respect and pride in net promoting itself . . . all that's crucial. But more than anything else, they have to be taught to teach others to succeed."

Wrapping Up

Astonishing. Everything was astonishing. The reality is, my life had changed 180° in merely 5 days.

It felt so excellent! You've all heard the secret for success a lot of times – and for some of you, hearing it has made an enormous difference in your lives – but for most of us, simply hearing about something isn't adequate.

Do you recall, as a child, how you learned to walk . . . or ride a bike? You were shown. Somebody put you on a bike and ran along beside you, holding the seat to keep it steady so you wouldn't fall off – and showed you how to accomplish it. "Looking back on it all, you may assume that what you thought you didn't know was the secret. That once you got that knowledge, once you learned that one thing you recognized that you didn't know yet, and then you rode your bike.

But if you think back really carefully, you'll discover that the secret to riding didn't come from what you knew – and it didn't come from what you thought you didn't know, either. That special secret lived someplace in a vast expanse of unexplored knowledge – what I've learned to call what you don't know that you don't know.

I'm telling you this about being shown . . . about what you don't know that you don't know because success, having success and doing successful things, is precisely like this. It is a state of being. "You're either being successful – or you're not. There's no in between.

If I were you, I believe I'd want to understand how it all turned out for me. It did – turn out, I mean, and as astonishing as it appears (at least it seems that way to me), it's all pretty much the way you'd anticipate.

It's what I do for a living today.

My Network Marketing business prospered from then on. A fairy-tale life – issue free? No way! The truth is, I've had more than my share of issues. But what if issues weren't good or bad? What if they simply were? And what if, because issues were merely things that occurred, we could make them into whatever we wished, whatever served and empowered us at the time? Are you questioning if I finally did buy his home?

Yes, I did.

I thank you for reading my book. And now, I'd like to share with you an easy secret for learning that's served me really well since it was first taught to me: Now that you've read it – read it again. And then, read it a third time. If you do read the book again, utilize it as a flashlight. There are thoughts, feelings and experiences "neatly scattered" throughout its pages, that will shine fresh light.

And then, ask yourself, "What's next for you?"

www.ingramcontent.com/pod-product-compliance
Lightning Source LLC
Chambersburg PA
CBHW070721180526
45167CB00004B/1571